BOOK ANALYSIS

Written by Hadrien Seret
Translated by Carly Probert

AF131398

1984

BY GEORGE ORWELL

GEORGE ORWELL

ENGLISH WRITER

- **Born in Motihari (Bengal) in 1903**
- **Died in London in 1950**
- **Notable works:**
  - *Homage to Catalonia* (1930), narrative
  - *Animal Farm* (1945), novel
  - *1984* (1949), novel

George Orwell (whose real name was Eric Arthur Blair) was an English writer born in 1903 in Motihari (Bengal). After being educated in England, he returned to India and joined the Imperial Police in Burma. He resigned in 1928 and decided to become a writer. He spent the following years wandering in Paris and London, where he mixed with the less fortunate (*Down and Out in Paris and London*, 1933). He then held various positions (librarian, teacher, and columnist) before joining the Spanish Civil War against the fascists (*Homage to Catalonia*, 1938).

During the Second World War, he devoted himself to journalism and writing his most famous novels, *Animal Farm* (1945) and *1984* (1949). Orwell died of tuberculosis in London in 1950.

1984

A PRAISE OF FREEDOM OF EXPRESSION

- **Genre:** dystopian novel
- **Reference edition:** Orwell, G. (2013) *1984*. London: Arcturus Publishing Limited.
- **First edition:** 1949
- **Themes:** totalitarianism, politics, freedom, war, utopia, collectivism

Contrary to what one might think, *1984* was not published in 1984, but in 1949. The work is a dystopian novel, a genre in which the author offers a vision of the future through their story. The vision proposed by Orwell is that of a world at war, governed by three superpowers. The author depicts one of them, Oceania, which is a totalitarian universe lead with an iron fist by Big Brother and his Party.

In criticizing a false society where nothing is permitted and where even the slightest deviation is sanctioned, Orwell is a reminder of the efforts of Winston Smith to fight the system with his memories and his love. The novel ends with the impossibility of making any changes and the destruction of the hero by the regime.

SUMMARY

A WORLD UNDER SURVEILLANCE

The action takes place in 1984, when the world is divided into three superpowers that are constantly at war: Eastasia, Eurasia and Oceania. The latter's capital city is London, which is led by Big Brother and his Party. The people there enjoy little freedom. Each inhabitant is constantly monitored by microphones and telescreens that can transmit information about the regime, as well as survey their every move. Anyone with thoughts adverse to Big Brother is immediately arrested and eliminated by the Thought Police. Moreover, from food to razor blades, everything is provided and controlled by the Party and its four ministries, which also regulate the amorous practices and Newspeak, the national language.

A Party official, Winston Smith lives in London and works at the Ministry of Truth, in the Record Department, where he is responsible for editing the history of Oceania or adapting it to recent events that have occurred. One day, during the Two Minutes Hate, a daily ritual where all officials shout their contempt for Goldstein and his small group of the Brotherhood, sworn enemies of Big Brother, he catches the eye of his colleague O'Brien: through it, Winston is convinced that another person thinks like him. He does not doubt for one second that this is a trap. From then on, every night when he gets home, he writes his memories and his hatred for Big Brother in a notebook.

IN SEARCH OF THE PAST

Despite his aversion, Winston Smith manages to live without his subversive thoughts being apparent. After finding a newspaper clipping that has not been edited by the regime, this gives him the ability to look for traces of the non-falsified past.

However, witnesses from this prior period are difficult to find: they do exist among the proletarians, a class containing the majority of the population, channeled and despised by the Party because a revolution of their part may cause its downfall. Winston only manages to get in touch with people whose memories are imprecise.

One day, while taking a walk, he visits the antiquarian Charrington and buys a coral clipboard. On leaving the shop, he realizes that he is being followed by a young girl with black hair who has been monitoring him for weeks. Winston immediately fears being denounced and captured, but the girl he believed to be a spy turns out to be a Party member. This young woman, Julia, is in love with Winston and, when he realizes his feelings for her, they both arrange to see one another in places where the telescreens and microphones are not likely to surprise them, and they give themselves to one another.

Looking for a safe place to express their love, Winston rents a room on the top floor of the antique shop. Hidden from every telescreen, the couple spends quality time together, despite the presence of rats which terrifies Winston. Although their situation is dangerous and precarious, it makes life more bearable for the hero, especially since he can speak freely about the past with Charrington.

THE BROTHERHOOD

One day, O'Brien takes advantage of a pretext to give his address to Winston. Winston then takes Julia to his house. There, they discover that O'Brien is an active member of the Brotherhood and offers them the chance to join him in his fight against the regime: they accept. O'Brien then smuggles Winston a copy of Goldstein's book in which the mechanisms of the Big Brother regime are explained.

But, in reality, O'Brien is a member of the Party and everything has been planned from the beginning: Goldstein and the Brotherhood have never existed, which Winston and Julia are quick to discover. Indeed, when the couple find themselves in the antique shop after a particularly grueling week, they are surprised by the voice of a telescreen hidden in the room. Charrington, who is actually an officer of the Thought Police, arrests and imprisons them. Winston is incarcerated and tortured at the Ministry of Love.

For O'Brien, it is crucial to love Big Brother and accept his version of the past: therefore, he wants to cure Winston of the hatred that he bears towards the head of the Party and of his attachment to the past. In order for Winston to fully assimilate the logic of the Party at the expense of his own, O'Brien makes him undergo various tortures, but he only partially achieves this result as Winston is attached to Julia, and refuses to betray her.

ROOM 101

To solve this problem and thus conclude his rehabilitation, O'Brien brings Winston to Room 101. There, faced with rats that eat his face, Winston ends up confessing everything, betraying Julia, who does the same on her part. Emptied of his original character, Winston is released.

A few days later, he meets Julia in a bar. Both of them have completely changed and no longer have any feelings for one another. They decide to break up. On hearing a news story on the telescreen, Winston realizes that he loves Big Brother. His recovery is complete: he can now be shot.

CHARACTER STUDY

WINSTON SMITH

A Party official, aged 39, Winston Smith works at the Ministry of Truth in the Record Department, where he is responsible for the falsification of the past on behalf of the regime. He was married to a woman, Catherine, from whom he has been separated for ten years at the time of the story. He is also Julia's lover.

The protagonist of the story, Winston quickly assumes the role of a rebel. His protest, which he knows to be dangerous, takes place in two stages:

- Denunciation in writing. By writing snippets of his past and his total rejection of Big Brother in his notebook, Winston automatically becomes an opponent of the laws and institutions set up by the regime. He is nevertheless aware of the illegality of his act, which is why he carries out this work out of range of his telescreen;
- Denunciation by adultery. By responding positively to Julia's advances, Winston is actively betraying the ideology of the Party. He maintains sexual relations with another person while still officially married and, even worse, he does so for pleasure. The special, yet risky, moments he spends with the young woman in Charrington's room are an opportunity for him to escape from the control and oppression exercised by the leader of Oceania for a few moments.

Imprisoned and tortured, he is cured of his hate for Big Brother, despite his resistance and his love for Julia. He is released some time later and subsequently shot.

JULIA

Also a Party official, aged 26, Julia works in the Fiction Department where she prints books on behalf of the regime. Like Winston, she has divergent thoughts concerning the Party and noticing this feature in the hero is what makes her fall in love.

Julia's rebellious actions are essentially based on the perception of her image by the regime. Thus, she participates in all of its associations, dedicating countless extra hours to the glory of Big Brother and presents herself as a relentless enemy of Goldstein. All this devotion to the Party allows her to attract sympathy, to the point of being made an example of. She then benefits from her reputation by breaking the rules, for example by sleeping with Party members and stealing food that isn't regulated by the regime.

Unlike Winston, Julia demonstrates a great sense of resourcefulness which allows her to develop tricks to escape the vigilance of Big Brother. Additionally, she is not at all interested in the non-falsified past: she knows the vices of the world in which she lives and simply wants to share moments of happiness with Winston.

Arrested at the same time as Winston, she also cracks under torture. Having considerably changed, she breaks up with Winston and she is not seen again.

O'BRIEN

A top member of the Inner Party, O'Brien is a mysterious and intelligent man. He is a member of the Ministry of Love, where his role is to heal those who have committed a crime against Big Brother. In 1984, he is of vital importance as the instigator of Winston's treachery and demise. Indeed, it is he who, by means of a look, pushes Winston to keep the diary in which he expresses his hatred toward the leader of Oceania. Having gained the trust of the hero through this process, he then uses his influence to trap him.

To do this, he makes him believe that he is a member of the Brotherhood, a small group headed by Goldstein, an enemy that wants to overthrow Big Brother. Having received the consent of Winston (and Julia) to join the fight, he completes the process by asking them to read a book by Goldstein on the operating mode of the system. In reality, Goldstein is nothing more than an invention of the Party to make its members more loyal. As for the book, it is a work of fiction written partly by Goldstein himself.

When he finds Winston again, O'Brien reveals himself as the one who will relieve him of his unhealthy thoughts that he holds against Big Brother. Despite some difficulties, he manages to completely convert him to the official ideology of the regime. His mission complete, he releases Winston.

BIG BROTHER

Big Brother is the Party leader and the leader of Oceania, although he does not really exist. He is an image invented by the Party to legitimize its possession of all power.

The inhabitants worship this icon of the regime, without knowing that it is a scam. This enthusiasm surrounding his personality explains the important role that he plays in their lives.

- Nothing existed before Big Brother, who is the past, present and future of Oceania.
- Big Brother is omniscient, omnipotent and he is also the source of all the blessings that exist in the country.
- His decisions are always the best and can never be questioned. It is therefore impossible not to love Big Brother.

To reinforce this sense of adoration, portraits of the leader are plastered throughout the city and the telescreens constantly launch slogans proclaiming his glory (e.g. "Big Brother is watching you"). Singing and celebrations also take place to pay homage to him (particularly in the Week of Hate).

In addition, any person experiencing negative thoughts towards him is eradicated.

ANALYSIS

1984, A DYSTOPIA OF TOTALITARIANISM IN 3 AXES

GOOD TO KNOW: WHAT IS DYSTOPIA?

1984 is often considered to be a novel belonging to the literary genre of dystopia or anti-utopia. This concept is the opposite to that of utopia: whilst utopia describes perfect society models, dystopia novels give a vision – usually futuristic – of a seemingly perfect society, which in reality is rejected as it makes life unbearable.

Drawing on his experience of the Spanish Civil War, Orwell wanted to propose a personal conception of what could become everyday life in a totalitarian state. He thus tries to evoke a society that could exist, without knowing whether this will really be the case.

Suppression of individuality

In Oceania, almost everything is done as a community: officials work together, eat together in the canteen and go together to the ritual of the Two Minutes Hate. In the evening, when the working day is over, they attend activities organized by the Party together. The Party even encourages them to work for free during their spare time.

This tendency to favor collectivity has two consequences:

- It oppresses all forms of creativity and individual thought: residents, by allowing the Party to govern their lives, become much more naïve and, therefore, easy to manipulate.
- Any personal action becomes suspicious and is liable to be denounced. This is why Winston must take extreme care when writing in his notebook or visiting Charrington.

Suppression of human happiness

Life organized by the Party is structured so as to eliminate any genuine happiness, i.e. all happiness of a human origin, as this can be a source of ruin for the Big Brother regime. Thus, sexual pleasure is strictly forbidden: the carnal act is reserved only for procreation in order to banish any feelings of contentment.

Another example can be found in the disappearance of any family or social links: everyone considers themselves to be comrades of Big Brother. Friends and family do not exist, and no one hesitates to denounce a relative if they betray the power.

The only joy that can be expressed by inhabitants are related to artificial satisfactions provided by the Party: pleasures obtained by the consumption of specific food (e.g. Victory Gin), by listening to good news on the telescreen or by endlessly worshipping Big Brother.

Suppression of freedom

A direct consequence of the suppression of individuality, the world of Oceania is characterized by a complete absence of freedom:

- There is no freedom of movement as the whereabouts of each person are monitored by telescreens and microphones.
- There is no freedom of expression as the only accepted view is that delivered by the Party. All negative judgment concerning Big Brother is considered a crime and is sanctioned by eradication. To avoid indiscretions, the power continuously removes words from Newspeak so that everyone is only able to speak well of the regime.

THEMES IN *1984*

Big Brother and the Party: themes of power and falsehood

As O'Brien reveals to Winston, the Party has set up a dystopian society with the sole aim of willingly being given power, which is to be used for its own purposes.

To achieve this goal, the regime first suppressed all forms of freedom and independence among the inhabitants, and then created an entity that was able to control them: this is the Party and its ministries.

With this totalitarianism installed, legitimations of this power were required. These are all invented and untrue:

- The state of war. From the beginning of the plot, Oceania is presented as a nation at war. The conflict seems lengthy and endless. In fact, there is no reason for its existence and it is simply caused by the regime to destroy its surplus production and population. Nevertheless, the different military victories announced by the telescreens serve to raise the people's enthusiasm for Big Brother's actions.

- Goldstein and the Brotherhood. The eternal and sworn enemy of Big Brother is also nothing more than a Party invention. This provides an opportunity to legitimize the security measures taken in the world of Oceania. Moreover, by providing a subject of hatred for its people, the Party strengthens the worship for its leader.
- Falsified past. As explained previously, the past is constantly modified by the Party, in order to support its existence and legitimacy in time and in practice. Thus, what people consider to be the true story is actually a lie orchestrated by the Party.

The utopia of a previous period: the themes of love and the true past

Another kind of past is developed through the character of Winston Smith. This is the past "before", the period that took place before the advent of Big Brother and which the Party wants to erase through falsification.

This true past is always presented in a positive way: whether through places (the "Golden Landscape") or objects (the coral clipboard), its beauty is always highlighted, as well as its incorruptibility by the regime. Orwell uses this as an expression of a better world which existed but which has been regulated to a forgotten utopia by the policy of disguise of the established power.

The specific and wonderful character of the past is strengthened by its role as the host of the love between Winston and Julia. Indeed, they express their passion in places that are steeped in history (the countryside and the antique shop, the latter being the ultimate place of memory).

Thus, the combination of this utopia and adultery, which, as already explained, is illegal, confirms Winston's impression that he is making a "political act" against the Party.

1984, AN ANTI-STALIN NOVEL?

In developing this dystopia, George Orwell was inspired by the dictatorship established by Stalin (Soviet statesman, 1879-1953) between 1929 and 1953. The many similarities that are found between the two powers, coupled with the pessimistic view put forward by the author, prompted many to consider *1984* as a critique of Stalinism.

At the time of the USSR, there was:

- Stalin, the leader of the Communist Party, who established a cult of his personality.
- The party office that applied the regime's policy with the help of its executives. The proletarians, indoctrinated, worked for its benefit.
- Propaganda for the regime. Films, pamphlets and books extolling the virtues of the power were produced. The idealized portraits of Stalin were distributed all over the Soviet Union.
- The creation of a secret police that repressed any rebellion against authority.

- Deportation of opponents to labor camps (gulags).
- Censorship. The regime resorted to censorship and editing to remove traces of the people that it executed.

In the novel, we discover that:

- Inhabitants worship Big Brother, the Party leader
- The Party holds all power in Oceania. The proletarians are nothing more than a mass that is controlled and neutralized by the regime.
- The Party controls everything that is produced on its territory. Propaganda is ensured through slogans ("Big Brother is watching you") and diffused through the telescreens. In addition, posters of Big Brother are plastered everywhere.
- There are telescreens, microphones and Thought Police whose role is to identify opponents of the regime.
- Opponents are sent to the Ministry of Love where they are tortured, brainwashed, then shot.
- The Party falsifies the past and deletes all information of those eliminated by the power from the archives.

FURTHER REFLECTION

SOME QUESTIONS TO THINK ABOUT...

- Explain the title of the novel.
- How does *1984* turns the past into a utopia?
- How does the Party legitimize its power? What do you think of these methods?
- Why did the loyal followers of Big Brother take the time to write the book by Goldstein? What interest and benefits can they derive from it?
- According to Orwell, "intellectuals are inclined to totalitarianism far more than ordinary people". Comment on this quote.
- Establish a parallel between the society represented in Orwell's novel and the totalitarian regimes that emerged in the first half of the nineteenth century.
- In another famous anti-utopia of the twentieth century, *Brave New World*, Aldous Huxley (British writer, 1894-1963) also imagines the future of England. However, the totalitarian society that he describes is not the same as that of Orwell. What makes the two different? Explain your answer.
- What similarities can be found between our society and that described in *1984*? Do you think Orwell's fictional society will become a reality one day?
- Do you think that there is a link between this work and the television program *Big Brother*? Justify your opinion.

We want to hear from you!
Leave a comment on your online library
and share your favourite books on social media!

FURTHER READING

REFERENCE EDITION

- Orwell, G. (2013) *1984*. London: Arcturus Publishing Limited.

REFERENCE STUDIES

- Aron, P. and Riot-Sarcey, M. (2004) Utopie. In Aron, P. Saint-Jacques, D. and Viala, A. *Le Dictionnaire du littéraire*. Paris: PUF.
- Calder, J. (1987) *Animal Farm & Nineteen Eighty-Four*. Milton Keynes: Open University Press.
- Galloy, D. and Hayt, F. (1994) *De 1848 à 1945*. Bruxelles: De Boeck Wesmael.
- Kadiu, S. (2007) *George Orwell - Milan Kundera: individu, littérature, revolution*. Paris: L'Harmattan.

ADAPTATIONS

- *1984*. (1956) [Film]. Michael Anderson. Dir. UK/USA: Columbia Pictures Corporation.
- *1984*. (1984) [Film]. Michael Radford. Dir. UK: Umbrella-Rosenblum Film Production.
- The novel has also been adapted for several theatre productions.

MORE FROM BRIGHTSUMMARIES.COM

- Reading guide – *Animal Farm* by George Orwell

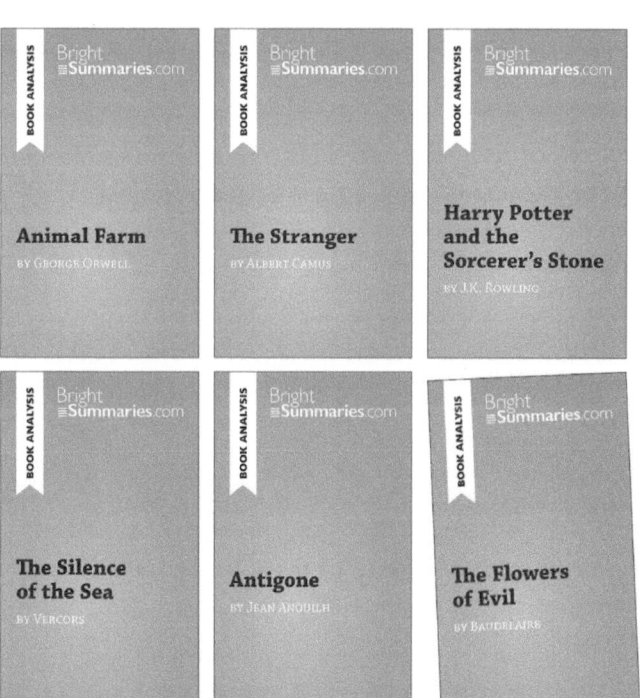